Look and See

A What's-Not-the-Same Game

by Bill Kontzias

Holiday House / New York

For Helen, Olga, and John

The publisher and photographer would like to thank Stephen Toth, rising third-grader, for reviewing this book.

Text and photographs copyright © 2014 by Bill Kontzias
All Rights Reserved
HOLIDAY HOUSE is registered in the U.S. Patent and Trademark Office.
Printed and Bound in November 2013 at Kwong Fat Offset Printing Co., Ltd., DongGuan City, China.
The artwork was created in camera, tabletop photography with simple lighting schemes, designed to tell stories with minimum computer manipulation.
The photographs were taken with a high-quality digital camera and two vintage film lenses that were modified and adapted to fit current technology.
www.holidayhouse.com
First Edition
1 3 5 7 9 10 8 6 4 2

Library of Congress Cataloging-in-Publication Data
Kontzias, Bill.
Look and see : a what's-not-the-same game / by Bill Kontzias. — First edition.
pages cm
ISBN 978-0-8234-2860-1 (hardcover)
1. Picture puzzles—Juvenile literature. I. Title.
GV1507.P47K68 2014
793.73—dc23
2013019678

How to Play

Look at the first picture.
Look at the second picture.
In the second picture, 1 thing is new,
1 thing is gone, and 6 things moved.
Find the differences. The answers are
at the back of the book.

On this page, a snake is **new**;
an elephant is **gone**; and a rhinoceros,
2 alligators, a big pig, a giraffe,
and a shark **moved**.

7 things are new,
0 are gone,
2 moved.

Prehistoric Look and See

7 things are new, 0 are gone, 4 moved.

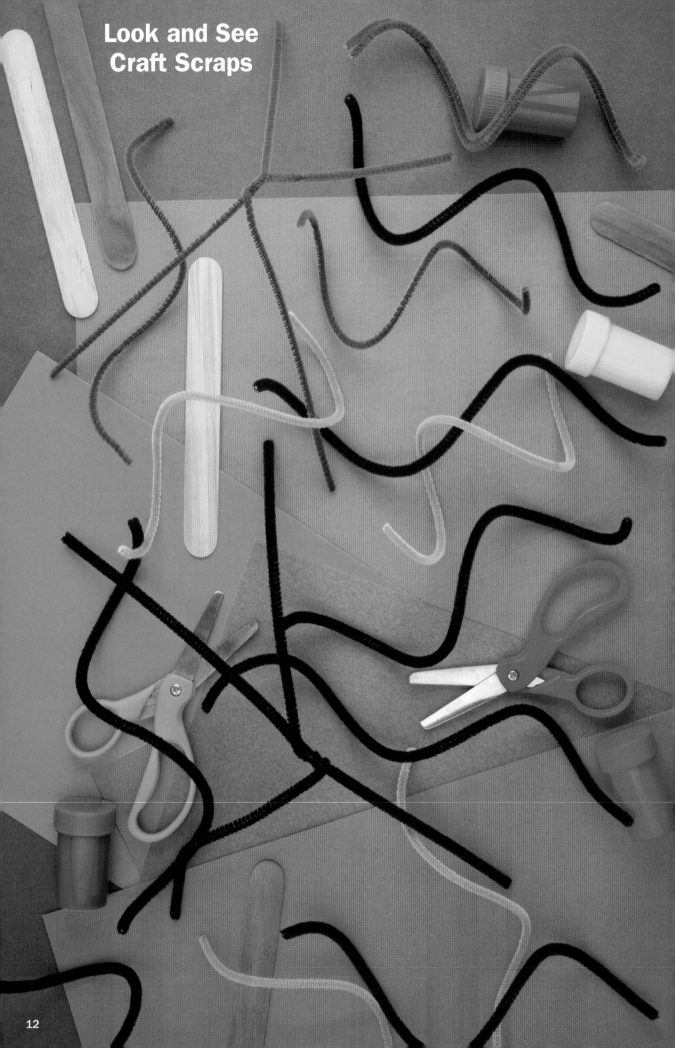

**Look and See
Craft Scraps**

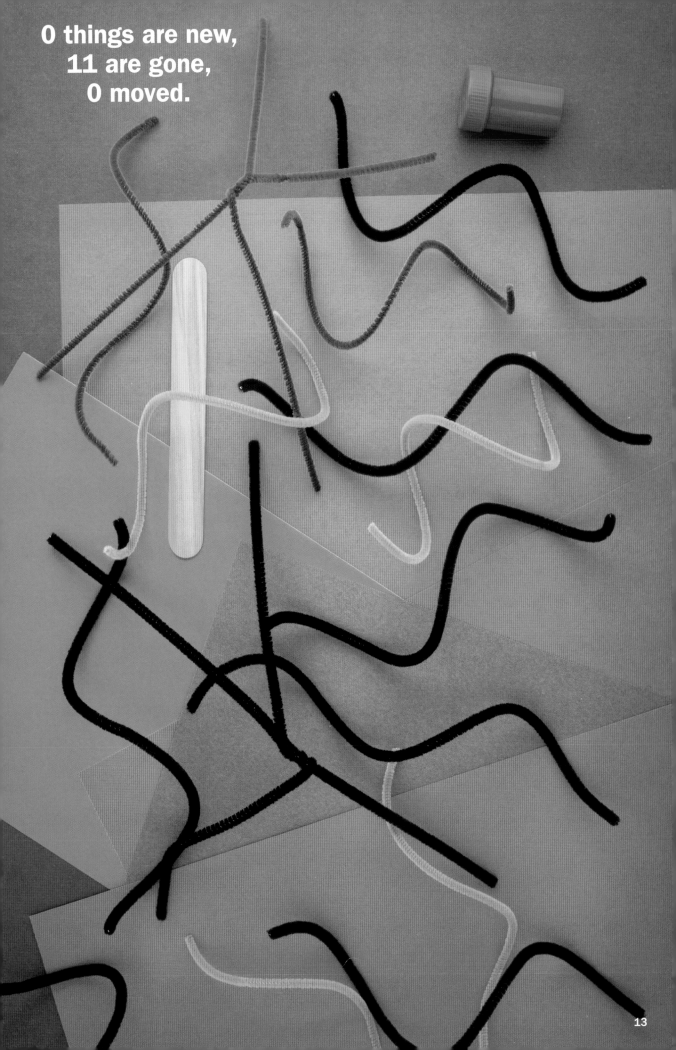

0 things are new,
11 are gone,
0 moved.

13

2 things are new, 1 is gone, 6 moved.

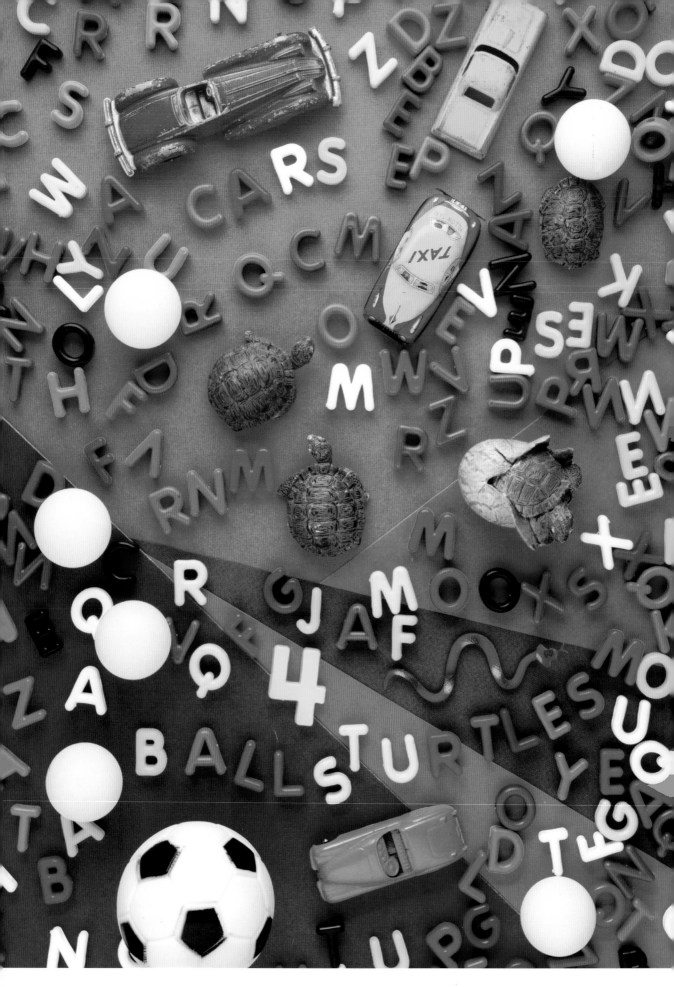

Look and See a Mess of Letters

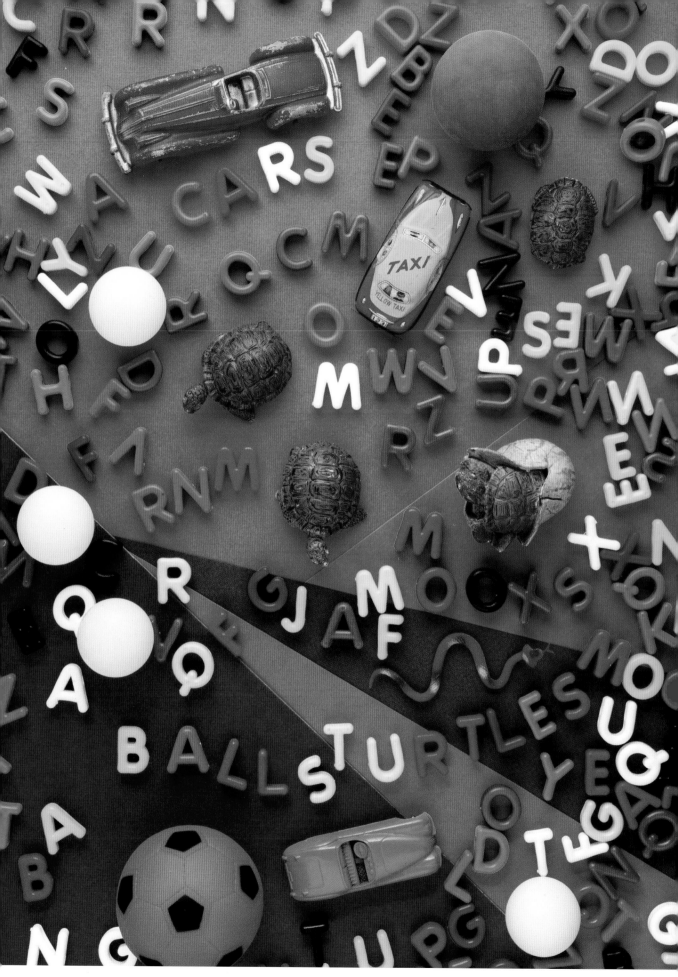

2 things are new, 5 are gone, 6 moved.

**Look and See
Birds and
Blocks**

6 things are new,
1 is gone,
3 moved.

Look and See Happy Faces

4 things are new, 7 are gone, 2 moved.

Look and See Metamorphosis

7 things are new, 5 are gone, 1 moved.

We ♥ Buttons Look and See

1 thing is new, 8 are gone, 4 moved.

11 things are new, 6 are gone, 11 moved.

Float and Fly Look and See

8 things are new, 3 are gone, 4 moved.

Look and See Shifting Shapes

7 things are new, 7 are gone, 7 moved.

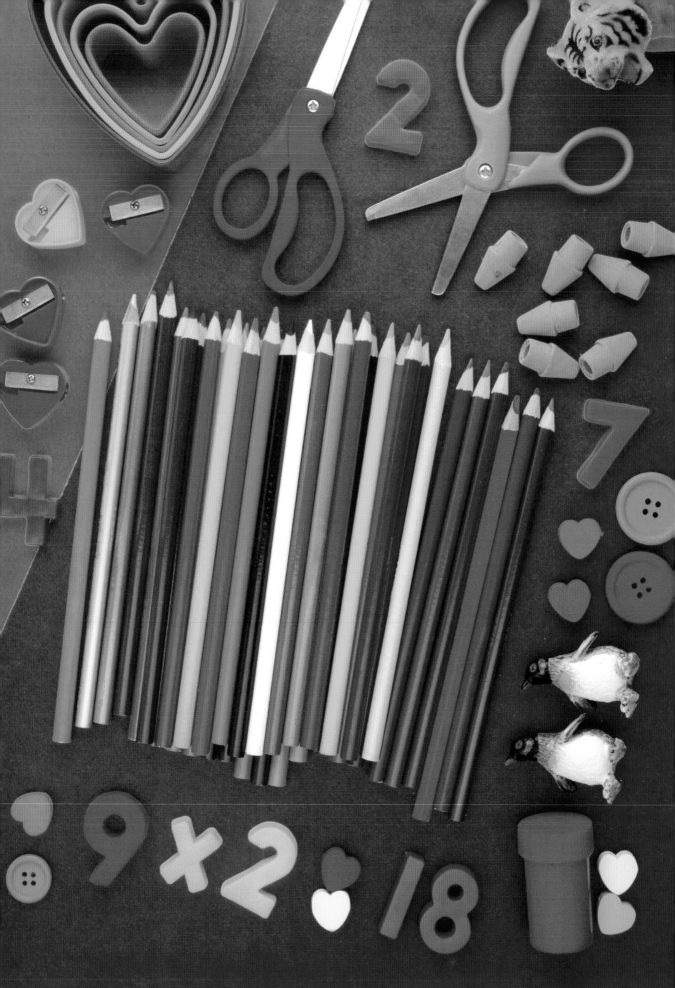

Color Full Look and See

11 things are new, 13 are gone, 0 moved.

More to Look and See

Puffs
Find 1 difference between the pictures on the front endpapers.

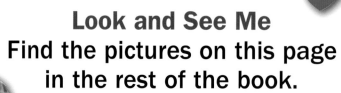

Pipe Cleaners
Find 1 difference between the pictures on the back endpapers.

Look and See Me
Find the pictures on this page in the rest of the book.
(No answers for this one. You're on your own.)

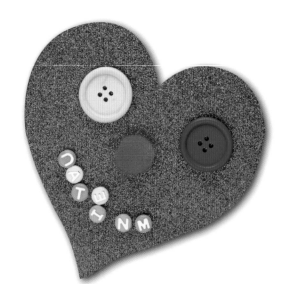

34

Look and See the Answers

From the Sea
New: ball, 6 shells. **Gone**: nothing. **Moved**: 2 shells.

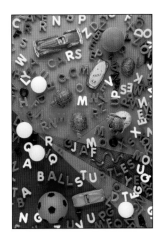

Mess of Letters
New: pink soccer ball, blue ball. **Gone**: white soccer ball, yellow *4*, 2 white Ping-Pong balls, yellow car. **Moved**: 3 turtles, red car, taxi, green car.

Prehistoric
New: 3 balls, 4 dinosaurs. **Gone**: nothing. **Moved**: 4 dinosaurs.

Birds and Blocks
New: bee block, 4 balls, yellow bird. **Gone**: red *O* block. **Moved**: 3 birds.

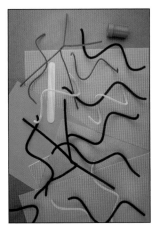

Craft Scraps
New: nothing. **Gone**: 4 craft sticks, 2 pairs of scissors, 2 green pipe cleaners, 3 paint bottles. **Moved**: nothing.

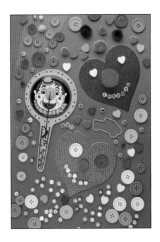

Happy Faces
New: small yellow button, car, white heart, blue button. **Gone**: red heart, pink button, big red puff, elephant, orange heart, small red button, yellow heart. **Moved**: big pink puff, little pink puff.

Safari Switch
New: gorilla's arm, big zebra. **Gone**: polar bear. **Moved**: 2 giraffes, tiger, hippopotamus, elephant, small zebra.

Metamorphosis
New: leaping blue frog, spotted red frog, 5 marbles. **Gone**: crouching blue frog, 2 salamanders, 2 rocks. **Moved**: marble.

We ♥ Buttons

New: diver. **Gone**: blue button, orange button, 3 blue hearts, white heart, orange heart, pink heart. **Moved**: blue button, green button, salamander, white heart.

Down the Road

New: 2 pigs, rooster-and-hen toy, tiny yellow truck, little red car, little blue car, 2 yellow blocks, horse, toy with 2 white geese, goat. **Gone**: blue car, red sports car, taxi, yellow car, green car, police car. **Moved**: red block, 5 red beads on abacus, 5 yellow beads on abacus.

Float and Fly

New: orange plane, bead turtle, 5 dice, sailboat. **Gone**: rubber raft, biplane, green-and-purple bead dog. **Moved**: parachute, diver, windsurfer, yellow plane.

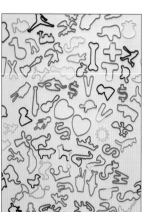

Shifting Shapes

New: large guitar, rabbit, heart, soccer player, sun, 2 heads and shoulders. **Gone**: yellow shoe, letter Y, purple fish, multicolored hippopotamus, blue rhinoceros, black dog, orange pig. **Moved**: bone, car, hand, girl, duck, 2 saxophones.

Color Full

New: large pink button, red number 3, polar bear, eraser, orange number 8, large blue button, zebra, yellow paint bottle, pink heart, purple number 7, yellow number 4. **Gone**: red paint bottle, red-handled scissors, orange number 2, 2 penguins, orange number 7, red button, small green button, orange heart, red number 9, purple number 8, purple number 4, red heart pencil sharpener. **Moved**: nothing.

Cover

New: yellow rectangle, green square. **Gone**: green triangle. **Moved**: nothing.

Puffs

A yellow puff is missing from the top, on the right.

Pipe Cleaners

A yellow pipe cleaner extends in the center, left.

ACKNOWLEDGMENTS

I would like to give special thanks to Grace Maccarone, for her encouragement and graceful critique; Betsy and Ted Lewin, for their true friendship, for their inspiration, and for mentoring this project; Kimberley McAdoo, New York City special education teacher, for sharing her insights and expertise; and Francesco Scavullo, my once-upon-a-time photography mentor, who remarked, "My dear William, visual problems are best solved visually. Your eyes are meant for seeing!"
—B. K.